Pebble® Plus

Plant Parts
Fruits

WITHDRAWN

by Vijaya Khisty Bodach

Consulting Editor: Gail Saunders-Smith, PhD

Consultant: Judson R. Scott, Current President
American Society of Consulting Arborists

Capstone
press®

Mankato, Minnesota

Pebble Plus is published by Capstone Press,
151 Good Counsel Drive, P.O. Box 669, Mankato, Minnesota 56002.
www.capstonepress.com

112009
005627R

Library of Congress Cataloging-in-Publication Data
Bodach, Vijaya Khisty.
    Fruits / by Vijaya Khisty Bodach.
    p. cm.—(Pebble plus. Plant parts)
    Summary: "Simple text and photographs presents the fruits of plants, how they grow, and their
uses"—Provided by publisher.
    Includes bibliographical references (p. 23) and index.
    ISBN-13: 978-0-7368-6343-8 (hardcover)
    ISBN-10: 0-7368-6343-5 (hardcover)
    ISBN-13: 978-0-7368-9620-7 (softcover pbk.)
    ISBN-10: 0-7368-9620-1 (softcover pbk.)
    1. Fruits—Juvenile literature. I. Title. II. Series.
QK660.B663 2007
575.6'7—dc22   2006000991

Editorial Credits
Sarah L. Schuette, editor; Jennifer Bergstrom, designer; Kelly Garvin, photo researcher/photo editor

Photo Credits
Capstone Press/Karon Dubke, 6–7, 12–13
Dwight R. Kuhn, 8–9, 15, 22 (tree)
Lynn M. Stone, 18–19
Robert McCaw, 16–17, 22 (blossom)
Shutterstock/Anne Kitzman, cover; Angelo Gilardelli, 11; Bezkorovayny Dmitry, 11 (pit); javarman, 22 (apple);
    John Said, 1; Olga Vasilkova, 4–5; Tom Oliveria, 21

Note to Parents and Teachers

The Plant Parts set supports national science standards related to identifying plant parts
and the diversity and interdependence of life. This book describes and illustrates fruit.
The images support early readers in understanding the text. The repetition of words and
phrases helps early readers learn new words. This book also introduces early readers
to subject-specific vocabulary words, which are defined in the Glossary section. Early
readers may need assistance to read some words and to use the Table of Contents,
Glossary, Read More, Internet Sites, and Index sections of the book.

Table of Contents

Plants Need Fruits

Fruits form from
the flowers of plants.
Fruits are soft and fleshy
or hard and dry.

Seeds grow inside fruits.
Fruits can have one seed
or many seeds.

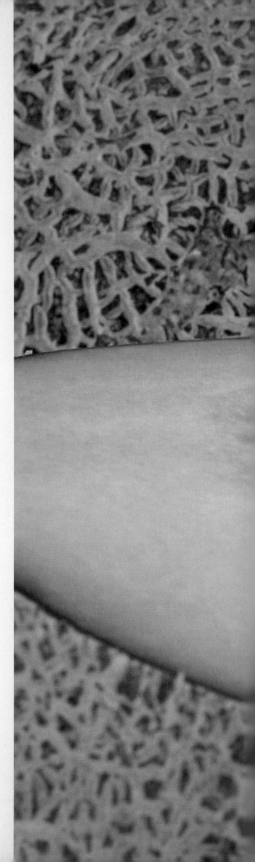

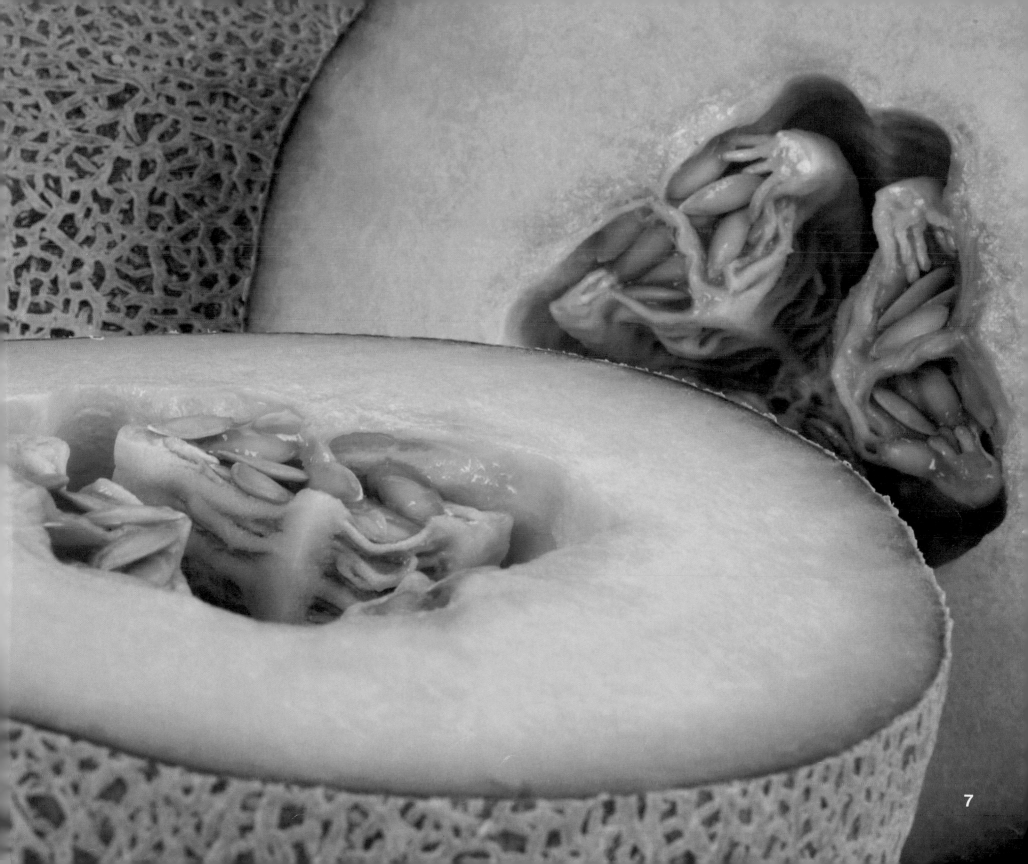

Fruits keep seeds safe.

New plants grow from seeds.

All Kinds of Fruits

Peaches are soft
and juicy fruits.
The hard seed inside
is called the pit.

11

Kiwi fruit has

many tiny seeds.

The black seeds are soft.

Acorns are hard fruits
with seeds inside.
Acorn seeds grow into
new oak trees.

Eating Fruits

We eat many fruits.

Blueberries are ripe

when they turn dark blue.

Oranges grow on trees
in warm places.
Oranges are squeezed
to make orange juice.

Wonderful Fruits

Sweet or sour, hard or soft,

fruits keep seeds safe

for plants.

Parts of an Apple Tree

flowers

leaves

seeds

fruit

stem

22

Glossary

flesh—the soft part of a fruit that you can eat

flower—the colorful plant part that makes fruit or seeds

pit—the large, hard seed in the middle of some fruit; peaches and plums have pits.

ripe—ready to be picked or eaten

seed—the part of a flowering plant that can grow into a new plant

Read More

Hibbert, Clare. *Life of an Apple.* Life Cycles. Chicago: Raintree, 2004.

McEvoy, Paul. *Plants as Food.* Plant Facts. Philadelphia: Chelsea Clubhouse, 2003.

Rondeau, Amanda. *Fruits Are Fun.* What Should I Eat? Edina, Minn.: Abdo, 2003.

Index

Word Count: 114
Grade: 1
Early-Intervention Level: 14

Internet Sites

FactHound offers a safe, fun way to find Internet sites related to this book. All of the sites on FactHound have been researched by our staff.

Here's how:

1. Visit *www.facthound.com*

2. Choose your grade level.

3. Type in this book ID **0736863435** for age-appropriate sites. You may also browse subjects by clicking on letters, or by clicking on pictures and words.

4. Click on the **Fetch It** button.

Facthound will fetch the best sites for you!